# Poet

## In The

# Street

### by Michael Porter

DE**V**ORA

PUBLISHING

JERUSALEM ◆ NEW YORK

## POET IN THE STREET

Published by Devora Publishing Company

Text Copyright © 2003 by Michael Porter

Illustrations and Cover Design: Janet Zwebner

Book Design: Tiffen Studios (T.C. Peterseil)

ISBN: 1-930143-76-1

Email: pitspop@netvision.net.il

Web Site  www.pitspopany.com

Printed in Israel

Thanks to Itamar,
   who said this would
      "perpetrate" into a book.

# TABLE OF CONTENTS

# AN EXPLANATION

Some of the most beautiful Hebrew songs I have heard are based on words taken from the Bible, and from the works of such Israeli poets as Bialik and Rachel. Other poetic songs I have heard were written and performed by the Beatles, Simon & Garfunkle, Bob Dylan, Joan Baez, and a handful of modern singers. The link between poetry and music is a strong one.

While the number of listeners to such music runs into many millions, when it comes to reading poetry we seem to be in another country altogether, a country which has few visitors.

Perhaps people are frightened off by the complexity of the "word game" involved in poetry. Words act as triggers which are supposed to lead the reader off into a maze of thought – his thought. And sometimes even the lovers of poetry find themselves wishing they had a "piece of string" to guide them.

What I try to do in this book is to give the reader a piece of string which will lead him or her to the entrance of the maze. Once there, they're on their own! Everyone responds to what he reads in his or her own way.

Which I think is what poetry is about.

# NATURE

*MY FIRST ISRAELI WINTER - COLD AND RAIN.*

*IN MY HOME-TOWN OF JOHANNESBURG IT RAINS IN SUMMER. I MISSED THE BUILD-UP OF HEAT DURING THE DAY, AND THE LIGHTNING WHICH WOULD SUDDENLY CRACK THE CLOUDS, BRINGING DOWN A SOLID WALL OF RAIN TO WASH THE STREETS AND COOL US DOWN. A WAVE OF HOMESICKNESS OVERWHELMED ME.*

*THE RESULT WAS A POEM*

## Summer Rain

At night the rain came
on running feet;
It sang a fierce song over the
fields of the sea,
its quiet scouts scoured the shores,
tapped their signals
upon our rooftops.

Timid houses stand submissive
under the downpour;
streaming streets overflow their banks,
create canals leading to wild waterways.

In a sudden hush we hear the deep thrum
of the earth's celebratory song –

Then a giant whip cracks on the street outside,
  sends air in agony through the sky
                    searing, tearing shredded smashed
shattered scattered clouds –

The gray night once lit by shiv'ring street lights
                    vanishes
in the violence of the summer rain.

*Israel, 1960*

*A WINTER SUNSET SENDS TINTED-ORANGE CLOUDS DRIFTING OVER THE LONG AND LOW GREEN CARMEL MOUNTAIN RANGES. IT ALL LOOKS LIKE A PICTURE PAINTED ON A CHOCOLATE-BOX. THE VIEW FROM THE LIGHTHOUSE ON TOP OF THE FRENCH CARMEL, WITH THE MEDITERRANEAN SEA STRETCHING BEYOND THE HORIZON, GAVE BIRTH TO THIS RATHER POMPOUS POEM.*

## Sonnet in Prose

When from the Carmel's edge I peep
down, rocky coast below, deep where the sea crimples
and throws a fretwork of foaming lace; crystal water
so clear that white and brown the rocks appear
scattered on the vasty ocean floor; overhead the birds
are tossed on thick swiftflowing air, playful wind
butts the sky;
clothing flutters in despair, like flags in a storm
which crack and tear –
    I see all this; and not only seeing, feel;
    and gazing more, my mind does rest and heal.

*FOR MANY YEARS THIS NEXT POEM STOOD QUIETLY AMONG THE OTHERS, AND WHILE I REGULARLY WENT OVER THEM, EDITING AND PRUNING, THIS ONE I LEFT ALONE — THINKING THAT IT WAS QUITE A GOOD DESCRIPTION OF THAT DAY OF RAIN IN THE DESERT. ONE DAY, AFTER ABOUT 6 YEARS OF RE-READING THE POEMS, I LOOKED AT THIS ONE AGAIN, AND A COLD SHIVER WENT THROUGH ME. WHAT WAS IT I HAD SAID! I WAS IN A TOMB, THERE WAS WEEPING OUTSIDE, AND I WAS ENJOYING IT? WAS IT MY SUBCONSCIOUS MAKING A STATEMENT. GOD ALONE KNOWS.*

# Security

Rain drums
on wet canvas just above my head,
Blankets heaped on the stretcher bed –
The tent is sag and soggy.

Under the elements,
      unafraid, enjoying
      the dark gray day
      weeping outside
I lie in my canvas tomb –
dry.

*EVEN WHEN YOU GET OLDER, AND IN MOST COUNTRIES WOULD BE PUT OUT TO PASTURE, YOU HAVE TO DO RESERVE DUTY IN ISRAEL— AN UNFORTUNATE FACT OF LIFE IN THE MIDDLE EAST AT THIS TIME. AT LEAST THE OLDER GUYS WERE ABLE TO STAND GUARD DUTY, UNLESS THEY WERE TOTALLY BLIND. HOWEVER, AS I FOUND OUT, GOOD EARS ARE INFINITELY MORE IMPORTANT THAN EYESIGHT. AND TO SEE THE SUN COME UP AFTER A LONG, LONELY NIGHT OF GUARD DUTY IS AN EXHILARATING EXPERIENCE.*

## Guard Duty

Cloud my brother,
earth, and father sky,
fellow-fool sun,
      is your day as full of wonder as mine?

For several hours I have been sitting under this great tree.
Somewhere up there, hidden, a small bird
      is singing to his world;
I didn't hear him till later tho'. – It was dawn.
Guard duty was over,
      but these thoughts were keeping me from sleep –

The night is dark enough,
but when you have to watch
it seems to have no end;

All things are unknown, the nearest shrub a mystery,
the wind a stranger who calls,
And your ears your only friends.
Hour after hour, each with its pebble minutes and
              fluid seconds

washing the world in an endless sweep and fall;
And there you sit, the unwilling center of it all,
an island in an alien sea;

– It has been night before, but still hope fades,
which makes the joy of greeting sweeter still: –

The shadows slowly deepen, shapes evolve,
the sky separates itself from the sleeping earth;
Great things stir and hum with joy;
A small bird chirps a question to the gray morning,
a worm turns uneasily;
The time of light has begun,
and the sounds which it brings. –

I stretch, yawn,
get up and go to bed –
and then I can't sleep because of these thoughts
struggling in my head
wanting to fly, wanting to be heard.

So I give in, get up again, sit under this tree,
write
          and after –
I knew the bird was there (didn't see it tho'),

Stretched out my arms
to greet you all –
Cloud my brother,
earth, and father sky,
fellow-fool sun,

Is your day as full of wonder as mine?

*I SUPPOSE I PASSED THIS SMALL TREE A HUNDRED TIMES AND NEVER REALLY NOTICED IT. ONE MORNING, AFTER A LIGHT RAIN, THE SUN CAME OUT AND THOUSANDS OF TINY DROPLETS CLUSTERED ALONG THE LEAFLESS BRANCHES SHONE LIKE STRINGS OF DIAMONDS. IT SEEMS WONDERFUL THAT NATURE, RARELY SYMMETRICAL, IS SO HARMONIOUS.*

# April Rain

**Tiny tree, bare branches upright**
**– diamond raindrops distil white light –**
**asymmetrical symmetry,**
**stands secret there**
**for all to see.**

# The Lemon Grove

The early-morning air gently touched my
chilled face
as I stepped from the street
and into the weed-strewn lot –
the remnants of a citrus grove.

Here and there small lemon trees displayed
large choice of sweet white blossoms
to buyer bees engaged in filling sacs;
the crowding blocks of buildings seemed to disappear
as I traced my way along a tiny path
glimpsed below leaf-clusters of friendly khubeza *,
and breathed the perfumed air;
and I wondered –

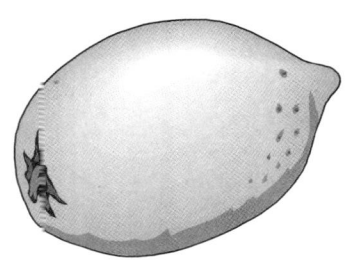

\* *Mallow*

18

when would someone realize the untapped potential
of this forgotten corner:
uproot the trees, send in bulldozers and cement mixers,
put up more buildings, fill his pockets –
and take away the choice from more than just the bees.

# JOKES, JINGLES, ETC.

I WONDER IF THERE ARE MANY COUNTRIES IN THE WORLD WHERE THE TELEPHONE — IN ALL ITS VARIATIONS — IS QUITE AS POPULAR AS IN ISRAEL. AS A NEW IMMIGRANT I HAD TO JOIN LONG QUEUES OUTSIDE THE DOORS OF GOVERNMENT OFFICES, WHILE THE CLERKS WOULD TOTALLY IGNORE US AND CHAT AWAY ON THE TELEPHONE.

MUCH OF THE MATERIAL IN THIS FOLLOWING SECTION IS NOT REALLY SUPPOSED TO MEAN ANYTHING. BUT WORDS HAVE A WILL OF THEIR OWN: THEY OFTEN REFUSE TO REMAIN MEANINGLESS.

# Jingle

Tho' the president may be in the middle of his thing,
　　in the land of Is-ra-el the telephone is king.
Lords, ladies, moguls, all jump at its ring,
　　in the land of Is-ra-el the telephone is king.
There's crowds outside the door, and some may be dying,
　　in the land of Is-ra-el the telephone is king.
On the verge of bankruptcy we may be tottering,
　　in the land of Is-ra-el the telephone is king.
For we never know what news the instrument may bring –
　　in the land of Is-ra-el the telephone
　　　　　　　　　　is king.

# Blind Men, Elephants and Fleas

We watched the road
stretching out before us.  Bad, bad, said she:
this reaching out is most suspect
in any self-respecting route.
Surely not, I heard him say,
Don't all roads behave this way?
That's not a road! said the child; I see
a playground waiting there for me.
- You are all correct;
it was the silent man talking –
so we continued on our way, and we saw
a dog chase a cat,
heard a crow caw.
We didn't see the fleas rolling in the dust,
but I'm sure
they saw all of us,
the dog, the cat, the people, the crow
as their next meal;
we shared in everything:
the road – the sun – the fleas –
the day.

*AT ONE STAGE OF THE GAME I WAS WORKING FOR A FRIEND IN HIS ICE-CREAM PARLOR IN JAFFA. WE BOTH WROTE POETRY IN OUR SPARE TIME, AND WE THOUGHT IT WAS A GOOD IDEA TO CHOOSE SUBJECTS AND WRITE ABOUT THEM. THE FIRST SUBJECT WAS (NATURALLY) ICE CREAM. THERE NEVER WAS A SECOND.*

# ce Cream I
# (as haiku)

**Child passes**
**small pink hand fingers**
**ice cream cone...**
**drops follow**

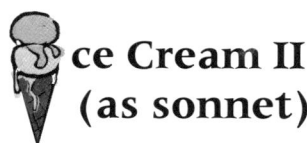

# ce Cream II
# (as sonnet)

How can I compare this taste,
these colors and this texture rare –
how can I state in words of haste
experiences beyond compare.
No, words of mine are dull to tell
the comfort and the joy it brings,
to draw upon this endless well
of cooling drafts and hidden springs.
'Tis better that I cease, desist,
and leave these lines to lesser men
who never had a taste of it
and therefore venture words; it's when
we've tasted of the cream of gods
our words and feelings are at odds.

# Tea for Itamar

For those who pace the halls of fame,
    and them wots on their way –
For those who wouldn't join the game,
    and them who waits the day –
For those who say: a damned shame,
    and them wot wouldn't say,
For those who always shift the blame,
    and them who always pay –

Along the corridors of time
this cry comes speeding down –
And we stop!!!
    Yea – the blinkin' lot o' us
from the lowest up; you see,
    we wants equality for all,
    but we also wants our tea.

# WRITTEN FOR THE OCCASION

# 1◯1 Ways to Treat an Egg

When first I cooked an egg, how proud I was;
I soon found to my sorrow, 9½ minutes is not 10,
and a 3-minute egg is not 3¼ minutes –
it seems I had stumbled onto an eggsact science;
So I burrowed into books about the egg,

found eggcellent recipes, which I tried
(all my little guinea-pigs died – I wonder why?
I followed all rules, quite dull and eggalitarian).

I started eggsperimenting.
With some eggstra effort I began
to turn out dishes eggstraordinaire',
even eggsotic:

28

only I couldn't find anyone to eat them;
The story about my guinea-pigs had been
grossly eggsaggerated – they all died peacefully.

If they bring me eggs to my padded cell
I don't eat them; I turn them decidedly down – I'm quite cool,
(they really think I'm some sort of fool..)
I must control my eggcitement – but
they're a mean bunch, egging on a drool
just because he's eggcentric.

# The Poet in the Street

Can you roar?  Coo like a dove?
Sing songs both of war and love? –
Pity... You were born too late.

The ancient days, now there's a time –
everyone appreciated rhyme. –
Those middle years were also known
for those who liked to hear a poem.  Today –
you're supposed to let it go,
to let your verses freely flow, to let it all hang out
so only the select few will know what it's all about:
those rather convoluted forces
which ink themselves as thought made word;
the main thing is to be heard –

though please, not too revolutionary,
we wouldn't want to scare the horses.

However, what this means:
writing for the occasion seems
out of date – very much so –
it vanished with the wind
which blew those years to long ago:

Who is the present poet laureate?
Does anybody know?

*VOICES IS AN UMBRELLA ORGANIZATION COMPRISING, IN SEVERAL CITIES IN ISRAEL, GROUPS OF AMATEUR POETS WHO MEET EVERY MONTH IN SOMEONE'S HOME. THE CHALLENGE HERE WAS THAT MANY OF US FELT WE HAD TO HAVE SOMETHING NEW TO BRING TO EACH MEETING. SOMETIMES, LIKE THE MACBETH OFFERING BELOW, THE POEM WAS WRITTEN BEFORE ONE'S TURN TO READ OUT SOMETHING — ANYTHING. AS LONG AS IT SOUNDED GOOD. ZORIKA, THE BEST POETRY READER I HAVE EVER HEARD, AGREED TO READ THIS — AND EVEN MADE IT SOUND GOOD.*

## Mr. & Mrs. Macbeth

Ah yes!  Macbeth and his lady:
the world was too much with him
(I know the feeling) –
all trouble, tribulation, toil and strife
and one ambitious wife:
It all adds up, the drive
     – and being driven –
to strive against one's kind
to please a lady.
Ah yes!  Macbeth: he got it all
and lost his peace of mind.

*SOMETIMES POEMS JUST WANDER ALONG UNTIL THEY WORK THEMSELVES OUT. AS I WAS TRYING TO TIDY THE NEXT ONE UP (READ — MAKE SOME SENSE OUT OF IT) A LAST LINE SUGGESTED ITSELF. WHETHER IT SUCCEEDS OR NOT IS ANOTHER MATTER. AND BY THE WAY, THIS BUSINESS ABOUT ONLY MAN HAVING A SOUL COULD WELL BE A FIGMENT OF HIS ARROGANCE.*

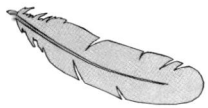

# Fellow Citizens

Do ants have heart attacks,
can birds get over-stressed?
City pigeons now
do they ever get depressed –
always on the move, forever fressing,
messing – to be brief,
   do they enjoy life's beauty!

Well, how can we know what's in another's life
which makes it act that way;
     For instance – do ants play?
  And chickens? – is there any light relief
from their pecking order?
How do city pigeons act
when they're off duty?

They don't read!
they don't write! –
yes, but do they think,
can they plan?

We know they're able
to spread their wings
    and fly away –
But do they understand
what a privilege this is –

Or is it all too easy!

# PEOPLE

# The Forgotten People

He was a garage worker in Tel Aviv,
a small old Arab man
who tried to save a girl
   –    a Jew:

they were both killed by the youth
    who used a butcher's knife.

In the market place in Jerusalem
a Jewish mother of eight
with her body shielded the Arab boy
who had stabbed, dropped his knife, and tried to flee.
"I could see he was unarmed" she said –
the angry mob attacked her instead; –
    she acted rightly, the rabbi ruled.

These are the people we will forget;
we only hear how bad humanity is –
   Yet
though we forget the name, the face,
the garage worker, the mother,
   the ordinary people –
they will always be there,
the unknown heroes of the human race.

*early 1990s*

*WHEN YOU'RE YOUNG YOU'RE USUALLY TOO INVOLVED TO NOTICE WHAT'S GOING ON AROUND YOU. THEN YOU GET OLDER...*

# The Cat Woman

Life is joy
desires
thrust of will
is good
is full –
love is not giving
or taking,
but sharing.
Trees bow
unobserved
the sun warms.

Now
she sits and
dreams; the cats
rub around her,
accepting swollen ankles.
Trees bow
unnoticed
the sun
does not warm old memories.

*I CAN'T HELP BUT ADMIRE PEOPLE WHO GROW OLD GRACEFULLY,
AND WHO HOLD TO THEIR DETERMINATION TO LEAD FULL LIVES.*

# In Praise of Old Age

My friend Harry Lieberman (we've never met,
but anyone aged 103 is my friend)
began his art career 23 years ago.
For 80 years he did not know
      he was an artist.
What I like most of all
is Harry's advice to the younger set:
"at 70 or 80, you should know
you're not too old", he says.

Rubinstein (it's like saying Shakespeare;
I mean no disrespect) –
at 90 plus the pianist sits erect
and plays the scores from memory,
his agile fingers, obedient still,
moving with an amazing complexity and skill.

My friend Yaacov David – and this time
it's someone I really met –
is quick and keen, as enthusiastic
as a boy. At 75
I hope I'll have half his drive,
and some of his enthusiasm,
and all of his health.

My father now, he doesn't like old age,
but, tho' he's 73
he's really younger than me.
His is an intellectual curiosity,
a direct approach, a clear mind;
myself, I take after my mother –
oi, how tiring
to be so young.

## Just a Man

Young Joseph Hillstrom
said: "don't mourn, organize"
    as he went out to be hanged.
The human spirit
    outlasts the man
        inspires nations –

There's a message here somewhere,
for those who want to hear it;
    Thank you Joe Hill.

# The Wheel of Fire

At this very moment that a baby is being born
  somewhere a man is being murdered,
  somewhere a nation is dying,
  somewhere new hope is springing up,
  somewhere people are mourning,
  somewhere a woman is being beaten,
  somewhere people are being robbed,
  somewhere someone is quietly doing a good deed,
  somewhere people go about their lives
          as best they can,
  somewhere people are making plans
          which will change the world.

Oh God, will there ever be an answer,
how will it all end –
  at this very moment a baby is being born...

*At a late age I started studying literature, and in less than a week I realized that much of what I had read up to that point I had lost. One of many revelations was the importance given to imagery and metaphor. The end of the day meant something more, and so did the shepherd. I had to pay attention.*

# The Shepherd

**At the end of the day**
**the shepherd approached his master's house**
**driving half his flock before him;**
**Where are my sheep, his master asked.**
**"Oh my Lord," humbly spoke the shepherd,**
**"they have strayed."**

# THE PROBLEMS OF
# BEING HUMAN

*Marriage must be the most difficult of all contracts to keep. Each side promises the other the same things: in other words equality – for the rest of their lives. Is this possible! Is it an experiment that, when things get tough, should be terminated? Is friendship a better foundation for a relationship? After all, friends accept each other as they are, and friendships are long-lasting (maybe because they don't live together!). Everyone interprets the marriage vows in his/her own way, one popular idea being that one becomes the "possession" of the other – that's not very friendly.*

# Wedding Anniversary

At the cafe Javonnaise
with all the high-class spenders,
and we, middle-class, not too smart –
    wedding anniversary
    and we live apart;
Twenty years is a lot of time together,
in 20 minutes over,
      and now
    we meet each week, and on occasion,
and speak – as if nothing has happened;
A great stretch of time has gone,
      is gone;
We pick up the pieces and try to make
a new puzzle to live by.

*IF PEOPLE WHO WANT TO SHARE THEIR LIVES COULD ONLY IRON OUT THEIR DIFFERENCES BEFORE THEY START THIS EXPERIMENT. IS THIS POSSIBLE! WE CAN'T KNOW WHAT'S IN THE FUTURE! OH WELL, ONE LIVES AND LEARNS: THAT'S WHAT LIFE IS ABOUT — I SUPPOSE.*

# The First Lie

A weariness washes over me,
springing from the mind;
it spills thru' the body, overpow'rs the limbs
stifles the senses –
I seek peace, sleep,
oblivion.
Should I have been prepared?
 It all began so quietly
 when you shared with me
 our first lie.

# The Betrayal

When its a mismatched marriage
kids are caught in the cross-fire:
oil and water don't mix –
oil is oil, water is water –
there's nothing wrong with either:
but go and explain this to the child
who only sees two parents – neither happy;
How unjust life is to the helpless young,
inevitably betrayed by the outgoing generation.

*Is a person alone when facing the realities of life, or is it possible to trust others? And if yes and no, when is it yes, and when is it no. To trust everyone is naive, and to trust nobody is cynical, and finding the happy medium is difficult. Perhaps it's safer to trust no one, but then risk losing something more valuable than safety.*

# The Jungle

**She looks at life with jungle eyes,**
**a struggle for survival;**
**she asks and gives no quarter, classifies**
**each one a latent rival;**
**In this both her strength and weakness lies.**

*THE MAN WHO SINGS "REGRETS, I HAD A FEW…" IS ONE OF THE LUCKY ONES. SOME OF US HAVE A LOT MORE THAN A FEW. SO WE TAKE NOTE OF THEM, LEARN WHAT'S POSSIBLE FROM THEM, AND THEN TRY TO FORGET THEM. IF YOU CAN'T LET GO, IT'S DIFFICULT TO GO FORWARD. WELL, WE KEEP ON TRYING — DON'T KNOCK IT!*

## Regrets I

Well, it seems
that I am made of words and dreams –
and that I don't know what to do
when they come true.

## Regrets II

I had the world,
the world I had before me.
And the world passed on –
and I remained.

# The Dream

I had a dream the other night –
that you were in my arms,
we danced upon the tops of trees
and balanced on the palms.
The moonbeams spun a silv'ry light,
the wind rode on the spray,
the stars peeped from a velvet night
and watched the world at play.

I had a dream the other night
that all the world was one;
and then I woke – the dream was o'er
and daylight had begun.

*ALWAYS IN THE BACK OF MY MIND IS THIS VAGUE REGRET THAT I DID NOT CHOOSE TO LIVE ON A KIBBUTZ (COMMUNAL FARM) — THE THING WHICH ATTRACTED ME TO ISRAEL IN THE FIRST PLACE. FOR INSTANCE, ONCE YOU EAT FRUIT YOU'VE PICKED OFF A TREE THERE'S NO BETTER WAY TO EAT FRUIT. THIS OCCASIONALLY LEADS ME INTO HOT WATER IN THE CITY WHEN I PICK SOMETHING OFF A TREE GROWING NEAR A BLOCK OF FLATS. THE RESIDENTS LEAVE THE FRUIT TO FALL ON THE GROUND AND ROT, BUT ALL THE SAME THEY DON'T WANT YOU TOUCHING THEIR TREE.*

*"SO WHY DON'T YOU PICK THE LEMONS" I ONCE ASKED AN OLD AND IRATE MAN. "IF I WANT LEMONS I'LL GO TO THE SHOP ON THE CORNER," HE SNAPPED. I DOUBT IF HE WAS EVER ON A KIBBUTZ.*

# Khaki Shorts

Yes
the grapefruit
     is good –
a bit sour;
now, at Beit Hashita *
we ate them off the trees –
grapefruit as big as melons:
even oranges were not as sweet;
or could the difference be
     the young man in khaki shorts
     who was eating them?

*\* A kibbutz in the Beit Shean valley, northern Israel.*

*MY FATHER'S FRIEND WAS ONE OF THESE COMPLETELY INDEPENDENT MEN. EVERYTHING HE WANTED, HE DID FOR HIMSELF. WHETHER HE READ, AND WHAT HE READ, I DON'T KNOW, BUT I DO KNOW THAT HE DIDN'T BELIEVE IN BOOKS. HE SAID IT WAS "READING OTHER PEOPLE'S IDEAS".*

# Mr. Mowbray's Philosophy

Let loose the louts of learning,
let them stumble and struggle in the morass of the
mind –
I know what I know!
What need to descant Kant, to mouth Shakespeare,
to quote what's his name;
Can you deny I stand here before you
on my own feet:
me, myself, alone,
Unafraid.

*AS WE GET OLDER THE ROAD SEEMS TO GET NARROWER AND TO LEAD IN ONE DEFINED DIRECTION. THE INEVITABILITY OF THIS COULD BE DEPRESSING — IF WE LET IT GET THROUGH TO US. AND IF WE DO, WELL — MAYBE WE CAN WRITE SOMETHING ABOUT IT.*

## Warning Light

When there is no returning
a small red light goes on –
          a warning!
From this point you're committed to the course.

   Up to this time
   there had been an option,
   you could go back and try again.

Now – only that red light
the rest of the way –
Let's hope like hell its the right one.

*I SAW THESE THREE YOUNG PEOPLE FOR LESS THAN A MINUTE,*
*AND YET THE IMPRESSION THEY LEFT WAS AN INDELIBLE ONE. AND THAT*
*QUESTIONABLE FEELING OF ENVY.*

# The Love Sellers

I saw three panthers in the street
sleek, proud, moving with absolute grace,
impeccably groomed;
The male more than six feet tall, tight T-shirt stretched
over bronzed and bulging biceps;
Two tall young women at his side,
short dresses, sheer stockings, high leather boots,
beauty personified.
They did not heed the mortals in the street,
this was a world they had discovered,
taken on their terms, conquered –
carved out their own paradise –
supremely content, supremely confident, supremely
sure –
I envied them. And then I realized
how right Milton was – evil shows a beautiful face.

# A BORING JOB

*WORKING AT A JOB YOU DON'T LIKE CAN LEAD TO THOUGHTS OF GLOOM AND PESSIMISM, WHICH EXPLAINS MOST OF WHAT FOLLOWS IN THIS SECTION. ACTUALLY, THAT'S WHEN THE POETRY REALLY BEGAN TO FLOW. DEPRESSION CAN HAVE ITS POSITIVE SIDE.*

# In the Fullness of Life

Is he crazy!
He's singing
actually singing
　　　while he works.

He doesn't know what a mess we're in?
doesn't he see there's no place to go
doesn't ...

he's still singing
on a building site
near the office.

At the moment everything is quiet;
soon enough the boss will show his strength,
start shouting at his staff –
one will be chosen and
run on command, like a wound-up toy.

Bored with the job
fed up with the boss
worrying about seeing the month out –
And this man's still singing!
Is he crazy?

*I WAS DEPRECATING A PAINTING I HAD DONE WHEN SUDDENLY I MET A PERTURBED PAIR OF BLUE-GRAY EYES, AND THE REMARK: 'THAT'S SINFUL'. OVER TIME I REALIZED THAT THE POSSESSOR OF THOSE EYES WAS RIGHT. BASICALLY THERE ARE TWO SORTS OF SINNERS: THOSE WHO SIN AGAINST OTHERS, AND THOSE WHO SIN AGAINST THEMSELVES. THE COMMON DENOMINATOR — EVERY SIN HAS A VICTIM. ARE SENSITIVE PEOPLE FOUND MORE AMONG THE SECOND TYPE OF SINNER? AND HOW CAN ONE SOLVE THIS PROBLEM? IT'S DIFFICULT TO CONSIDER STRONG NEGATIVE FEELINGS WITH IMPARTIALITY (I.E., HOW ON EARTH DOES THIS HELP ME?), BUT IT MIGHT BE A GOOD START.*

*THERE CAN, OF COURSE, BE A POSITIVE SIDE EVEN TO NEGATIVE FEELINGS. THE GREAT THING ABOUT TURNING ONE'S DEPRESSION INTO A WORK OF ART, FOR INSTANCE, IS THAT YOU GET INTERESTED IN WHAT YOU CREATED, AND THIS LIFTS YOU OUT OF THAT FRAME OF MIND WHICH INSPIRED YOU TO CREATE WHAT YOU CREATED. HMM! IS THAT CLEAR?*

## Sonnet of Self-Indulgence

I have been here too long,
it was a small song I had to sing,
it was not enough to be a man –
We do not fit, the world and I;
when all I touch is wrong,
and nothing but trouble do I bring,
no matter what I do or plan –
Is this the cue to say goodbye?
I did not ask, was this the fault?
I did not plan before.
I had no base, no wealth, no vault,
nor walls, nor neither door;
And yet, how strange: I do not know
another way that I would go.

# Killing Time

The corridors of life
are littered with the corpses of dead days
bleeding time:
And now another bloody day killed!

# TOWARDS THE FUTURE

*DO WE REALLY BELIEVE THAT THE WORLD IS A GLOBAL VILLAGE?
IT SEEMS RIDICULOUS NOT TO. THE JUNGLES BURNING ON SOME OTHER
CONTINENT AFFECT OUR LIVES AND THOSE OF OUR DESCENDANTS. THE
WARS, WHICH EVEN THE VAUNTED UNITED NATIONS CANNOT CONTROL,
TOUCH THE LIVES OF MILLIONS, CREATING DEATH, FAMINE, ILLNESS,
REFUGEES SPILLING OVER BORDERS. THE POLLUTION WE ARE GUILTY OF
REACHES AROUND THE GLOBE, AND THE SUN BURNS US ALL.*

# Looking at the Future

I looked into the round luminous eyes
of a starving child
filled with wonder and amazement,
not understanding this strange world
into which he had been born a few short years ago
and which he was soon to leave;
you well-fed mortals, you money-making machine-men
have you ever looked into the eyes of a starving child.
It's not really worth anything –

I looked into the unmoving eyes
of tiny skeletons
lying on the makeshift beds of war-torn hospitals,
not grasping the peculiar world
into which they had stumbled for such short space of time;
you well-fed mortals, you money-making machine-men
have you ever thought of looking
into the eyes of a dying child.
It's a risky business –

I looked into the unseeing eyes of a tiny child
sitting alone, deserted in the vastness of an empty place
his little back straight, his tears mindlessly flowing,
not understanding a chilling world
in which he would always be a stranger
(if by some stranger chance he should survive);
you well-fed mortals, you money-making machine-men
did you ever see an abandoned child.
There's nothing in it for you –

I tried to look into the eyes of small skeletons still walking
for that short space of time
left to them
and I turned away
while wondering what this peculiar place was
which people call the world, and why did we let it happen
and why did I turn away
and why was I so helpless.
You well-fed mortals, you money-making machine-men
have you ever looked at walking skeletons
and, like me, turned away.

I looked into the haunted eyes of an alien child
hiding from his enemy in filthy alleys,
accepting the horror of a world
into which he had been thrown
and which did not want him –
and I saw man's future.

You well-fed mortals, you money-making machine-men
have you ever seen man's future.
Perhaps it's better not to:

You might even believe there's something you could do;
bring some drops of hope to a chosen few
in this sea of misery
which we fondly call the world;
and this sort of thinking
might make you feel uncomfortable –

*THE OLDER WE GET THE MORE WE BECOME AWARE THAT THE NEXT GENERATION INHERITS WHATEVER WE LEAVE BEHIND — WHETHER IT'S SOMETHING DONE OR NOT DONE. SOME PEOPLE CAN'T HELP WORRYING ABOUT AN UNPREDICTABLE FUTURE, AND THE CHILDREN WHOSE LIVES WE ARE INEVITABLY INFLUENCING.*

## Towards the Future

He saw
a runaway truck
rolling down the hill,
and ran into the road
to stop it.

Get out of the way, people cried,
you can't stop it, you'll be killed –

He ran,
he shouted:
"Don't you see
    there are children inside!"

## Last Call

When the human race is run
and the battles' lost and won
and killing beams stream from the sun
and this poor earth at last undone –
then for a miracle we'll call,
and if there be none – God help us all.

# QUESTING

# Shedding Life's Fleas

**Many of life's problems
come to a man like fleas to a dog, which make
him bite his back until he bleeds.**

**If we're wise we wouldn't grieve too much
but rather rise
into the colder air –
It's easier to shed fleas there.**

*WE ARE BORN INNOCENT AND HELPLESS. THEN LIFE TAKES OVER, TEACHING US WHATEVER WE CAN ABSORB. IN THE EARLY YEARS WE ARE AT OUR MOST IMPRESSIONABLE — AND THESE YEARS WILL INFLUENCE THE REST OF OUR LIVES. IF WE'RE LUCKY WE'VE HAD GOOD TEACHERS. IT'S RARE THAT A PERSON THINKS THAT PERHAPS THERE IS SOMETHING "WRONG" WITH WHAT HE ACCEPTED AS A CHILD, AND THEN WILL TRY TO DO SOMETHING ABOUT IT. AND IF HE DOES TRY — CAN HE SUCCEED? WHO KNOWS! BUT BEING AWARE IS A ALREADY A TREMENDOUS STEP FORWARD.*

## Chain

Here we sit at the bottom of the sea
wrapp'd around with a childhood chain;
The ship's still sound, but hard aground.
Let's wait for the tide –
          a swelling wave –
to set it floating free again;
But can it break this childhood chain
which drags us down to the bottom of the sea?

*I TRIED TO WRITE SOMETHING USING AS FEW LETTERS AS POSSIBLE. WHAT EMERGED INSISTED ON GOING ITS OWN WAY.*

## Puzzle

Where were we
ere we were here?
Were we?
Are we aware we are here?
Are we?
Beware!
We are here,
but where is here,
and why?

We are aware,
but what is that –
and why?

We are...
weary...

*WE DRIFT IN AN OCEAN WHICH WE DEFINE AS "SPACE" AND "TIME". WE MOVE THROUGH "AIR" AS A FISH MOVES THROUGH "WATER". WITHOUT DOUBT WE ARE PART OF IT. YET MANY OF US FEEL AS OUTSIDERS — OUR RATIONAL SELVES DEMAND ANSWERS, BUT OUR EXPLANATIONS DON'T SATISFY US. SO — WHAT IS THE PURPOSE OF, SAY, AN ANT, A FISH, A CAT, A TREE, A BUTTERFLY — OR LIFE?*

*THE POEM BELOW SOUNDED RATHER WEAK, UNTIL I FOUND A SOLUTION, A FAIRLY SIMPLE ONE — I MOVED THE WORD "AND" FROM THE BEGINNING OF THE FOURTH AND EIGHTH LINES AND ATTACHED IT TO THE END OF THE LINE PRECEDING IT. IT CHANGED THE RHYTHM OF THE POEM, MAKING A BIG DIFFERENCE.*

## Wind and Ocean

The winds stir the ocean
the waves run their course,
they break on the shore, and
          return to their source.
Where do they come from
and where do they go?
The ocean remains, and
          the winds they do blow.

*HOW CAN A POET KNOW IF WHAT HE SAYS IS TRUE, EVEN THOUGH HE MAY FEEL IT IS? I'VE NEVER MET A RICH POET, BUT THIS DOESN'T STOP THE MIND FROM IMAGINING WHAT A RICH MAN SHOULD FEEL LIKE. WHEN YOU THINK ABOUT IT, IT SEEMS STRANGE THAT A MAN WITH LOTS OF MONEY WOULD WANT MORE AND MORE. IS IT POSSIBLE TO WANT SOMETHING YOU'VE ALREADY GOT? DEEP DOWN IS THAT WHAT HE REALLY WANTS? BUT THIS QUESTION OPENS UP A WHOLE NEW CAN OF WORMS, AND I DON'T HAVE AN APPETITE FOR IT.*

# Wanting I

**The man who has a quiet life
wishes he had a bit more money;**

**the man with a bit more money
would love it to be a million;
the man with a million
desires 10 million
the man with 10 million
Desperately needs 50 million.
The man with 50 million
wishes he had a quieter life.**

# Wanting II

Suppose, just suppose, it was as you dream
stretch out your hand, receive your every wish
eternal gold, eternal life, the best of
comforts, your every whim –
there would be no need for desire:
not to strive, not to cry, never to want;
Those with much would have more
Those with nothing would have all –

We would not *want*...
We would *not* want!

*A GIFT HAS ITS OWN DYNAMIC. IT IS SOMETHING GIVEN FROM ANOTHER SOURCE. BEFORE YOU GET THE GIFT YOU HAVE NO CONTROL OVER IT. ONCE IT'S YOURS YOUR CONTROL IS, USUALLY, ABSOLUTE. YOU CAN DO WHATEVER YOU WISH: USE IT, CHERISH IT, IGNORE IT, THROW IT AWAY, DESTROY IT — THE PRINCIPLE IS THE SAME WHETHER THE GIFT IS MONEY, AN IDEA, OR LIFE ITSELF.*

## The Gift

**When I was very young
my aunt gave me a gift –
'Michael, enjoy it,' she said.
Being a polite boy I offered her a 'thank you' in return;
Only now I realize with what great care,
with what love and hope
the gift was chosen –
the rest was up to me.**

*SOME PEOPLE ARE SELF-CRITICAL ALL THE TIME, AND SOME NEVER QUESTION THEMSELVES. I DON'T THINK EITHER ONE OF THEM IS DOING HIMSELF A FAVOR.*

*A RULE OF THUMB I USE FOR ANY ACTION WHICH RAISES A DOUBT — DOES IT HARM ANYONE (INCLUDING ME), OR DOES IT HELP ANYONE (INCLUDING ME). THIS SOUNDS TOO SIMPLE — AND IT IS. BUT TO ASK A QUESTION IS ALWAYS A GOOD BEGINNING. THEN COMES THE HARD PART — WHERE DO YOU GO FROM THERE?*

*THE BIBLE TELLS US, EVERYTHING IN MODERATION. THAT'S A HELP.*

# Self-Criticism

**I've seen too many singular things
not to be aware
that the faculty of self-criticism
is both precious and rare.**

# THE END OF DAYS

*IN ISRAEL MORE PEOPLE DIE ON THE ROADS THAN IN WARS, AND YET THE PUBLIC GENERALLY PRESENTS AN APATHETIC AND INDIFFERENT FACE. IT'S THE SELF-CENTERED ATTITUDE AGAIN — "IT ISN'T ME". A DANGEROUS WAY OF THINKING. WE ARE ALL INVOLVED. BUT BY THE TIME SOME PEOPLE FIND THIS OUT, IT'S TOO LATE.*

# On the Road

**Young lad in your leather jacket,
jeans, helmet, well-polished boots;
(the toes point up, the legs asprawl),
the motorcycle still under the truck;**

an ambulance is waiting.
We slow down; we see a faceless sheet,
            and polished boots,
toes pointing to the sky –
my boy's at home I hope:
it's someone else's son, someone else's brother –
I don't think he made it to husband or father.

We drive on – momentarily sobered
from our impatient way,
willing to wait that extra second –
now we've seen its power.

In the evening we pass again;
once more the road is clear.

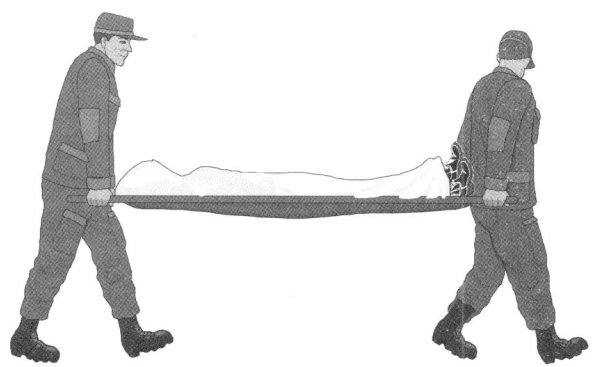

# The Bystander

And were you standing aside,
young, unknowing, standing aside
when a speeding car turned, overturned
from the road to the sidewalk, killed you
      unaware
            quickly
                  instantly!

It left shocked onlookers, police,
the ambulance, siren screaming;
but you were not aware.
And were you standing aside!
      young
            unknowing
                  standing aside!

*FAMILY MEMBERS AND A BUTTERFLY – UNITED IN THEIR DEATHS. IS DEATH AN ABSENCE OF LIFE, OR DOES IT HAVE ITS OWN MEANING? ANOTHER QUESTION WITHOUT AN ANSWER. YOU BELIEVE OR YOU DON'T BELIEVE. WHICHEVER WAY YOU DECIDE, THIS IS THE COMPASS WHICH WILL GUIDE YOU THROUGH LIFE. AND AT THE END... THE BIG QUESTION-MARK?*

## Butterfly on the Road

Thin wings folded in beauty
still intact, but closed,
the body crushed flat – on the road.
I try to take the butterfly
but the wind whips it from my fingers;
traffic streams endlessly by –
I go inside and wash my hands.

*WHAT BEGAN AS A GLOOMY AND INTROSPECTIVE POEM, OVER THE YEARS WORKED ITSELF INTO ANOTHER DIRECTION. HOWEVER, MORE THAN 8 YEARS OF EDITING HAS NOT MANAGED TO CHANGE THE RAMBLING NATURE OF THE POEM BELOW.*

# A Gift of Gold

I have thought about death,
that final jest –
that contract that we, unwilling,
drew up when we were born.

I have thought about death – my death,
of not being; of... nothing more... and
this thought has turned me cold and desperate.

    I have thought about death –
    the ordained end from which we cannot flee –
    And the solace of religion
    does not weigh with me.

I have thought about death – my death,
and of those before, and after,
who died, and will die too:
and that I am one with them
comforts me.


My grandfather
 – now no more –
told his children:
"when I die, don't mourn –
    have a party."

A scholar who fled his native land
he found freedom on a feral shore;
he lived boldly,
he lived well,
prospered in his business, and

later –
after he had lost everything –
each day,
early each morning,
he would walk down the mountain road to his little
shop,
happy and contented with his lot;
        enjoying what he had, giving it meaning.

        So tell me – what does life mean?
    So, tell me, do you enjoy life?

What purpose has life until we live it;
what meaning has love until we give it;
what challenge can there be in fate unless we dare to
bend it;
what value can there be in time unless we spend it!

Life begins with the gift of gold
freely given: no one need ask;
But with the passing of each day – as the store grows
less –
are we more careful about the price we pay
for each pledge, with every task?

Some things we now begin to fathom:
        when we stray from gen'rous nature,
        we fall and drown in a sea of sorrow –

we belong to her; to betray this pact
warps our will: it will twist our very fiber –
And at the end of the day: the contract holds;
the debt is still there to defray.

So why do we worry this bone of contention
which was resolved with our first breath;
when life needs so much of our attention
it's folly to still think of death.

# Sorry!  No Exceptions

No – you're trying to bend me, death
and I don't think it's a good idea;
I want to enjoy life while it's still here –
be a good chap now – stay on your side of the fence.

You've sent one of your faithful followers,
the quiet one,
to discuss the matter with me –
sorry to say this, but I don't agree.
Yes yes, I know, I'm lucky to meet old age –
so many people never get to this stage –
but to tell the truth, I'm not quite ready.

Oh!  You don't make exceptions.

*FINDING NAMES FOR THE UNKNOWN GIVES US A FEELING OF COMFORT.*

*THE UNKNOWABLE BECOMES THE NAME. WE BUILD RULES AND STRUCTURES AROUND IT, AND WE FEEL EASIER IN OUR MINDS. WE ARE COPING! SCIENTISTS, MATHEMATICIANS, CLERGYMEN, POLITICIANS, WRITERS — IT DOESN'T MATTER WHO: WE ALL DO IT. AND SOMETIMES WE TALK TO OURSELVES.*

**Sebastian**

**It's getting harder to ignore
that fellow standing there behind the door,
staring through the hollows where his eyes should be,
waiting to serve me –
I shall call him
Sebastian.**

# Esther

We stood in mud among the graves
and heard his voice, the song of sorrow,
while the body, so shrunken under the sheet,
was given to the patient soil.

Who were you, and what?
A housewife, a quiet woman,
almost, almost unnoticed;
all these things – the children grown,
the home swept clean, food always there –
all these things you gave unseen,
quietly, and almost, almost unnoticed.
You were ill for many years;
a small woman, you became still smaller,
until the offering to the earth
was almost, almost insignificant.

We mourn, we live, we forget –
      a pebble dropped in the pool
      settles as quietly to the floor –
but the heavens wept.

*Esther Yeremiash, Haifa  January 1, 1981*

# My Father

We come, we go,
joys and sorrow,
yesterday, today, tomorrow
      passed, passes, will pass,
And at last we will be left
behind, while time moves on.

And there was a sound of thunder,
      and great rocks split asunder,
      and a mighty wind came –
      and then a still, small voice.

I will listen well to the quiet sounds;
      the humming of the earth,
      the silent shout of sun,
      the patter of rain,
   the sound of the human spirit –
      a life lived
in joy and pain,
      a still, small voice
      whispering the meaning
ever_asting.

*Jack Sellick Porter, November 1, 1984*

## Le'haim!

For three months now
we had been watching Zvi die
in this last, final hospital,
always somebody at the bedside;
Saturday night, a call, we were all there
in the darkened room, watching the shrunken form
gasping for air,
waiting for a sign;

And Zvi sat up – where is the wine, he said;
his daughters sped away, returned
with glasses and a bottle, gave him wine;
it was a moment of joy, strength flowed in the man
he raised his glass to us – Le'haim! (to life), he said,
Le'haim! we answered, and drank.
Early next morning, as the sun came up,
Zvi died.

**Zvi Yeremiash, September 21, 1992**

# POLITICS AND WAR

*AS A NEWSPAPERMAN I HAVE SEEN AT FIRST HAND WHAT POWER AND EFFECT WORDS HAVE ON MEN. THE POEM BELOW IS A RECOGNITION OF THE PART POLITICIANS PLAY IN USING WORDS FOR THEIR OWN PURPOSES, AND YES, I DID HAVE SOMEONE IN MIND WHEN I WROTE IT.*

## Words

There's those that walk in high and heady air,
and carelessly, or not, dislodge a pebble here and there,
and obediently the little fellows roll, all starting slow,
garnering here a friend, another there, as down they go.
If, say, someone below would cast a glance
above him, and act quickly, there'd be a chance
that he might stop an avalanche, but this is rare –
those busy with their daily toil have little time, we fear –
until, the noise so loud, at last the danger's clear;

however, by this time, there's nothing can be done;
those little fellows soon cover everyone –
except for those that walk in high and heady air
and carelessly – or maybe not – throw down a pebble
here and there.

# Those Who do not go to War

Young lives pay
for mistakes the old men make –
the power that corrupts
does so whether subtly or no,
and the old one who survives
is corrupted, whether subtly or no.

These are the elected,
these are the leaders of men,
these are the ones we trusted,
the ones we wished for – and got –
and once having, cannot shrug off.

But in the homes
wait the bereaved –
each life had so many roles,
father, husband, son, brother, friend –
the loss is the end, there is no more
for those who wait... they wait...
                    there is no more.

Why don't we think it strange
that the men who die are so young,
and the politicians are so old?

*THE NAZIS WERE PROUD OF THEIR MURDERS, KEEPING METICULOUS RECORDS AND DOCUMENTS REGARDING THEIR VICTIMS. PHOTOGRAPHS TOO.*

# And Now, in this Century

### *(Both poems are based on photographs taken in Nazi Germany)*

We were chosen, so I'm told,
we were chosen to bring
the Word of God to a godless world.
We did not choose.
         .   **But why choose us?**

Perhaps because we are an enduring people –
and the bringing of the Word is an endless task.
        **Because we shall endure?**
        **Because of this!**

The soldier raises his rifle
        and shoots.
One bullet is for the child,
the second for the mother who holds him.
The soldier shoots.
        **Can he shoot the Word of God?**
        **Does he kill that which gives him life?**
He pulls the trigger
        and he shoots into the body of his family.
He kills,
        and he kills his own.

# A Day in the Country

An open place: the air is quiet;
trees abound, and grass, and flowers,
the sun is bright, birds sing somewhere;
Soldiers rest in the open glade –
waiting for their orders.
Two machine guns are loaded, ready.

Officers stand with serious faces,
man's work is to be done –
meanwhile, they wait,
wait for the right moment.

A small distance away
a group of naked men huddle together –
and wait.

# Holocaust Day

The sirens sound; we stop
stand a moment, pray,
think of a continent of people killed;
children who saw the day
   for the last time;
      And –
What have we learned!
Why has this been
the age of the holocaust!

Is man unaware
of the deadly seed he carries within!
This most tragic of all disease,
like the plague,
crosses continents and seas;
Waiting –
and always ready;

have we not seen with our own eyes
the corruption of those who embrace
depravity –
slipping down a never-ending slope
they only see that simulated face
which shrouds the poisoned well
and ultimately destroys all hope.

What can the fight against evil bring
if evil has no end;
only that he who yields to it
   loses everything!

*ONE CAN'T SAY ANYTHING POSITIVE ABOUT THE FIRST GULF WAR,
ESPECIALLY FROM AN ISRAELI PERSPECTIVE. TAPING UP THE WINDOWS,
WEARING GAS MASKS (EXCEPT THE DOG, BUT HE CAME ALONG QUIETLY),
COOPED UP IN A SEALED ROOM UNTIL THE ALL-CLEAR AND THANKING
GOD YOU'RE ALIVE TO HEAR IT, IS NO WAY TO END THE DAY. BUT IT MADE
GOOD TELEVISION.*

# Encounter at Mach 5

High overhead two lights lazily float
    toward each other
    across the quiet night,
locked in an inevitable encounter
at mach 5 –
a tribute to technology.

They meet,
    they set the air on fire,
and then they flicker out
      above the naughty world;
the red-hot metal
like passion, quickly cools,
falls back to earth,
and dies.

*Tel Aviv 1991*

## The Promise I

Who can fail to be moved by this lovely day;
the trees display their buds, and promise future blossom,
soft breezes promise an end to winter's sway,
no clouds mar the blue of the sky –
birds sing busily as I pass by –
the earth rejoices, the soil after rain
smells of freshness, a promise of new life –
people sitting in a bus early this morning
were blown apart by a bomb –
soon the jacarandas will be showing gentle flowers.

*Tel Aviv March 3, 1996*

# The Promise II

Was yesterday a beautiful day!
Today I see the mimosa
bursting like yellow sparks from the bush,
woodpeckers trill out their song
and tap secret codes on the bark.

The strelizias, like elegant cranes with
long orange beaks
peer proudly from amongst green leaves,
and that harbinger of spring, the loquat tree
shows oval green fruit;
this day was more successful for the madness of man
another bomb, this time in a busy street,
killed little children as well.

*Tel Aviv March 4, 1996*

*THIS IS A RECURRING THEME — THAT THE SCOUNDRELS OF THIS WORLD ALWAYS MAKE LIFE MISERABLE FOR THOSE WEAKER THAN THEMSELVES. FOR ME THE THIRD WORLD WAR IS THE ONE BETWEEN TERRORISTS AND CIVILIANS. WE DON'T HEAR OF TERRORIST GANG X AND TERRORIST GANG Y FIGHTING EACH OTHER — CIVILIANS ARE THEIR PREFERRED TARGETS. THE BOOTLEG GANGSTERS OF CHICAGO WERE FAIRER; THEY KILLED EACH OTHER AS WELL.*

## The Murderers Among Us

What screw is loose in humankind!
What deadly vapors do we find
in the ooze and sewers of our mind!
The century has witnessed
                such outrages,
dead, dying, dispossessed
men, and women, and children –
sheer numbers exceeding all other ages.
        In some future they will wonder,
    could this all be true;
    was homo sapiens capable of such depravity?
Did he really devise such subtle toys
    making murder oh so easy
    in the hands of overgrown boys?

Refugees flee
across a disintegrating world –
their numbers exceeding all other ages;
        Even the expulsions of the Jews
            was not in tens upon tens of millions
        and nowhere to turn – at least they had their sages.

98

The principle here,
    which cuts across all continents and all ages –
This mindless void, the killer's endless will for blood,
    his desire: to purge the "different" one
        from his small time in the sun –
        to strip him of his very life – is twofold,
    the victim's helplessness, the killer's fear.

The murderer's choice of victim
        is someone weaker than himself;
            a savage commonsense
    breathes in this freak –
he gives good reasons for his evil,
except for one: that he's a man afraid;
he fears life,
he fears death,
he fears the other,
he fears himself.

He is that part of mankind which strives
with such great passion
to drag us back into the primeval slime...
        His contribution to life
            is death.

And yet – humanity endures, moves forward slowly,
        a silent, suffering majority
        cutting across all continents and all ages –
Nothing changes.

*AS A BOY IN SOUTH AFRICA I ACCEPTED WHAT I HEARD AROUND ME — JEWS ARE DIFFERENT. MANY YEARS OF LIVING IN ISRAEL SHOWED ME WHAT A FRAUD THIS WAS — ISRAELIS ARE A PEOPLE LIKE ANY OTHER (CAN I EVER FORGIVE THEM!). THEY COME FROM ALL PARTS OF THE HUMAN SPECTRUM. ROUGHLY SAID, THE WORLD DIVIDES INTO THREE TYPES OF PEOPLES — THE TWO EXTREMES, AND THE OFTEN-SHIFTING MIDDLE GROUND. THE IMPORTANT THING IS NOT THAT THE EXTREMES EXIST, BUT HOW SOCIETY RESPONDS TO THEM.*

# The "Uber" Man

*("They scorned us just for being what we are"*
*– from the song 'Galway Bay' )*

Probably
the unrivaled hoaxer of history:
      the victimizer –
           revealing a seeming honesty –
           permits his victims to take the blame;

Whether the Red Indian, the Bushman or Aborigine,
or Armenian, or Chinaman, or Gypsy or Jew
   – or any different other –
it really doesn't matter who;
it becomes another reason
   why arrogance should show no mercy
   for his weaker brother.

The "uber" man, behind his solid wall,
safe from the sweep of sympathy,
knows the problem lies outside:
his proof is that he feels no shame;

he is sure!
Right is his when might is his –
he is the final arbiter;
no truth prevails but his desire,
that he may be the hangman too.

And so, when with him strides the night,
how can he abide an eternal day!
And those who commit the mortal sin
of grieving for this mindless man
will they pass away?

*TO FIND REASONS IS SIMPLE. TO GO DOWNHILL IS SIMPLE. THE ROAD ONLY GETS EASIER. TO GO UP AGAIN IS A STRUGGLE. WHICH BEGS THE QUESTION — WHY IS THE RIGHT WAY ALMOST ALWAYS THE DIFFICULT ONE?*

## Reasons

**The man with evil on his mind
will always find good reason for his intent;
One doesn't need a reason to do good.**

*IF EVER A MAN COULD HAVE CHANGED THE FACE OF THE MIDDLE EAST THAT MAN WAS YITZHAK RABIN. HOLDING THE GOVERNMENT BY SHEER WILL AND HIS CHARISMA, HE DROVE AHEAD TO A FUTURE WHICH HELD OUT HOPE AND PROMISE TO ALL THE PEOPLES IN THE REGION. AND THEN A YOUNG MAN WITH A GUN PUT A STOP TO ALL THIS, DESTROYING THE HOPE AND BRINGING DISASTER ON US ALL. THIS WAS WRITTEN ON THE SECOND ANNIVERSARY OF RABIN'S DEATH.*

## The Soldier

**He fought in every war
but the enemies of Israel could not kill him;
it's when he fought for peace
that they succeeded.**

*November 4, 1997*

103